WORDS TO LIVE BY

Orley Herron, Ph.D.

STEPHEN AUBRY PUBLISHING CO.
EVANSTON, ILLINOIS 60201

STEPHEN AUBRY PUBLISHING, CO.
2840 SHERIDAN ROAD
EVANSTON, IL 60201

Printed in Canada.
10 9 8 7 6 5 4 3 2 1

ISBN: 1-889555-02-9

To Chase, Grant and Glenne....
My Loving Grandchildren

This book could not have been written without the tender and precise care of my associates, Kathryn Cody, Vickie Eckart, Jenny Dreyer, and Mary Harris. Their words of encouragement kept me to the task and cheered me on when writing became difficult. They are choice people.

The satisfaction you receive from the fulfillment of a task may be more important than the satisfaction you seek as you do the task.

Be a friend to yourself. That friendship may be the finest you will ever know.

People so often see you for what you can give to them rather than who you are.

Who you really are is what you must give to others.

Life does not owe you anything.
However, life needs your generosity,
never your selfishness.

Living life fully is a must, not a maybe.

Being accountable for your actions is the beginning of maturity.

Maturity is a process, not an instantaneous revelation.

You are responsible for you.

What others do or don't do should never be a priority on your personal agenda.

Gossip is the insatiable food of critically spirited people.

The high road is the only road to take.

Words should lift the spirit and help guide the way.

Words should be as warm as the sunshine of midday and as kind as the parent of a long awaited newborn child.

Words should be carefully chosen, kindly spoken and wonderfully remembered.

Your words should be a gift to others, cherished long and treasured often.

Eliminate words that hurt and destroy. Add words that heal and give new life.

Close friends are rare.
Keep them close.

Accept the loss rather than always wanting to replace it.

Loss can help you to reevaluate your priorities.

Memories that are good can start with each new day.

Learn to discern when to accept the situation rather than trying to change it.

Trust yourself, believe in yourself, and act for yourself with kindness and humility.

Others may need you more than you need them.

Helping others may help you help yourself.

Remember you must care for yourself before you can care well for others.

Burning yourself out in the care of others leaves you nothing to care for others, or even to care for yourself.

The guardian angel you seek may already be guarding you. Be at peace and be at rest!

Keeping up with the Joneses could be generational.

Whatever happened to the words "please" and "thank you"?

Blaming others for your faults only adds to your faults.

Eating everything in sight will hinder your need to be physically out of sight.

Always allow the facts to supersede your emotions with any difficult problem.

Most uses of anger are detrimental to the human spirit.

Frustration may be in conflict with wise decision making.

Being used by people may be a prerequisite of your vocation or your position.

The appetite for things may never be satisfied if not curbed early.

What habituates you may be what governs you.

Being quiet is becoming a lost art.

Acceptance may be a greater virtue than trying to change a situation that is not worth the effort in the long view of life.

Taking the longer and wider perspective may be better than the shorter and more narrow approach.

When one says, "Think before you speak," it may be a hint that your words are ineffective.

Remember words can draw people to you or drive them away. So select them carefully.

Recapture your childlike sense of awe when you see nature's beauty.

The snowflakes of winter are a white blanket of rare beauty and a spectacular creation. Enjoy them well.

Friends asking to help you may have a great need to fulfill. Allow them that pleasure.

The darkness of night should turn you to the brightness of the stars and the magnificent glow of the moon.

Allow the coming of night to usher for you the beginning of rest and restoration so you can anticipate the dawning of a new day with its challenges and opportunities.

When the facts state that once you are born you are also beginning to die, they do not mean that you must stop living and being a productive, caring human being.

When you are enjoying life, time moves by so quickly. Don't miss a second of its joy.

Conflict can drain you;
resolution can mend you;
forgiveness can restore you.

What you want to do and what you can do may be closer and more compatible than you can ever imagine.

Seize the opportunities. They may not come your way again.

Courage and fear are partners, not enemies.

Take the risk. It may be the best step you ever take.

Saying yes to the risky things and no to the wrong things are keys to successful living.

What others desire of you may not be what is the best for you or of you.

The storms in life may create beautiful rainbows of blessings.

Enemies are never in your best interest.

When you realize that people will mainly look out for themselves, then you will know how to look at them, when to look at them, and what to look for in them.

Friends may rarely give of their best. You must show them the way.

Children can teach us once again to see what we have long forgotten in our fast paced society. Allow them to do it now, and you will see the loving and creative things again in your journey of life.

Resting is always better than quitting in life's undertakings.

Remember you were young once. Allow the young to be young and enjoy the glory of youth.

Old age will come soon enough. Don't usher it in early in your thinking patterns and life choices.

Do you dread the end of each day? Then start enjoying the beginning of each day and never let that spirit of joy stop.

May the music of the night fill your day as well.

Life does not deal you bad choices. Bad choices are only options that can be changed, reshaped and redirected, if you are willing to put the effort to them.

Are you looking in the right places for your special destiny? It's there for the finding.

Discouragement can be conquered if you do not allow it to conquer you.

Hope is there for the taking, the receiving and the seeing. In fact, it may be just a breath away.

Life’s struggles are life’s special fitness programs.

Sorrow need not overwhelm you, but will build you up in greater love, greater tenderness, and greater compassion for others.

Patience is always a better choice than impatience in the development of relationships.

Tomorrow is a new day for you to enjoy and fulfill. Don't waste it.